LIFE IN ANCIENT CIVILIZATIONS

# The Greeks

## LIFE IN ANCIENT GREECE

by **Michelle Levine**

illustrated by **Samuel Hiti**

M Millbrook Press • Minneapolis

MACEDONIA

Mount
Olympus ▲

GREECE

Troy

Ionian
Sea

Aegean
Sea

Thebes

Athens

Corinth

Sparta

MEDITERRANEAN
SEA

CRETE

■ ANCIENT GREECE
● city-state

# Introduction

The people of ancient Greece lived more than 2,500 years ago. The ancient Greeks were curious and creative. Their greatest thinkers changed people's ideas about the world and their place in it. The Greeks are also known for their temples, their sculptures, and their style of government.

Ancient Greece was based in modern-day Greece. This country is in the Mediterranean region. It is the meeting point of Europe, the Middle East, and Africa. Over time, Greece came to include many settlements in these lands.

The people of ancient Greece left behind pottery, buildings, writings, and artwork. These remains tell us much about the way the Greeks lived.

# CHAPTER ONE

# Life in a Greek Community

Ancient Greece was made up of hundreds of small communities. These communities were known as city-states. A city-state included a central city and the countryside around it.

Each city-state had its own government and laws. Most city-states had five thousand or fewer citizens. Athens was the most famous city-state. It was also the largest. As many as three hundred thousand people lived there.

Many of ancient Greece's greatest artists, writers, and thinkers lived in Athens.

People in the city-states were divided into different classes, or groups. Wealthy landowners and business owners were part of the upper class. Upper-class families lived in big homes with large courtyards. The middle and working classes included traders, sellers, craftspeople, and farmers. Their homes were not as big as upper-class homes.

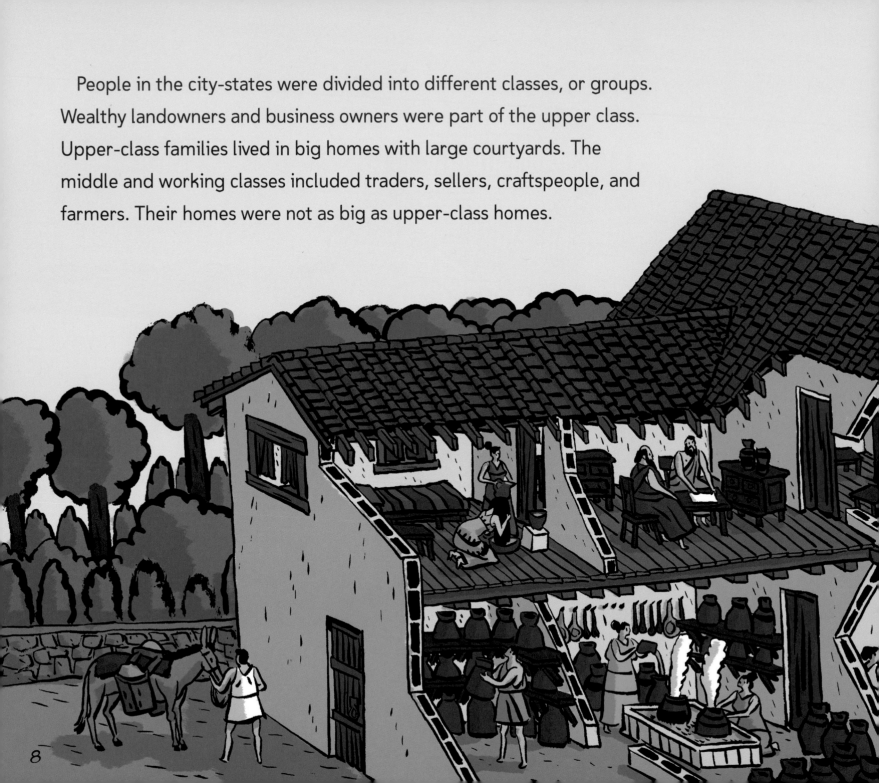

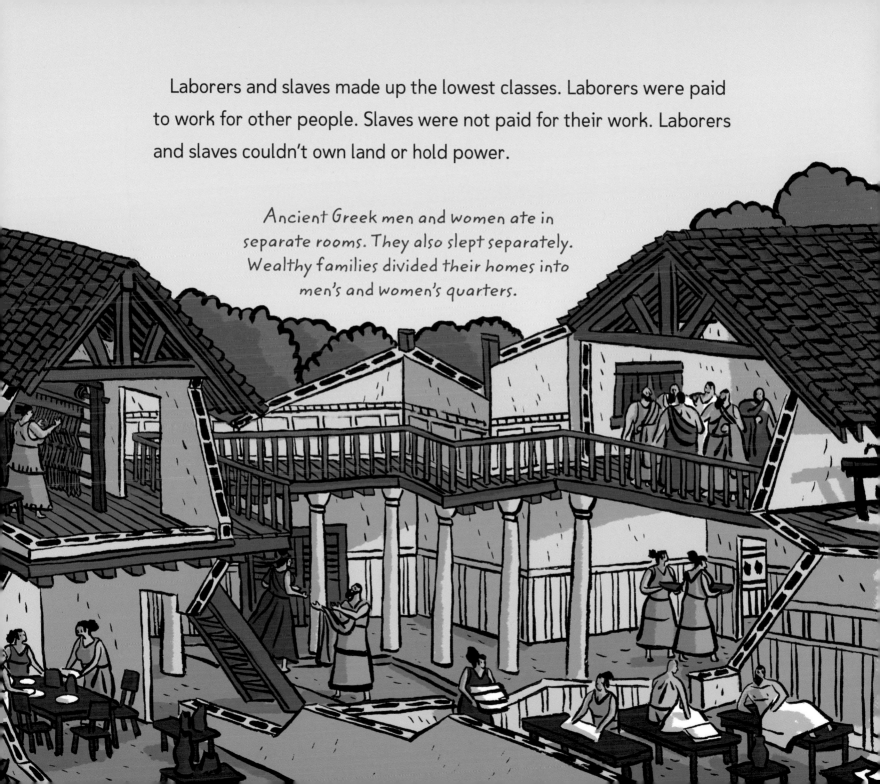

Laborers and slaves made up the lowest classes. Laborers were paid to work for other people. Slaves were not paid for their work. Laborers and slaves couldn't own land or hold power.

Ancient Greek men and women ate in separate rooms. They also slept separately. Wealthy families divided their homes into men's and women's quarters.

All Greeks shared the same basic diet. They ate the foods that grew best on Greece's hilly land. The most common foods were beans, goat cheese, bread, fish, and fruit. Many foods were cooked in olive oil. Wine was the Greeks' favorite drink.

Eating and drinking were part of many gatherings. One kind of gathering, the symposium, was a party. Upper-class families had symposiums in their homes. Only upper-class men were invited. The men rested on couches. They drank wine mixed with water. Dancers, singers, and poets entertained them. Sometimes the guests had serious discussions.

Ancient Greek pottery was often decorated with scenes from everyday life. This vase shows men gathering olives. Olives and olive oil were important in Greek cooking.

The ancient Greeks did not have forks. They used their fingers or bread to scoop food into their mouths.

Greeks wore simple clothing. Both men and women wore a loose piece of cloth called a chiton. Most people wore plain wool or linen chitons. Wealthy citizens dressed up in colorful silks. They pinned the chiton together at their shoulders. Children and slaves wore shorter chitons. Some people wore the chiton with a belt around the waist. Others wore cloaks over their chitons.

Many people wore sandals. Others went barefoot. Either way, the Greeks did a lot of walking. Travel by horse or donkey was rare. People usually traveled by boat to go to faraway places.

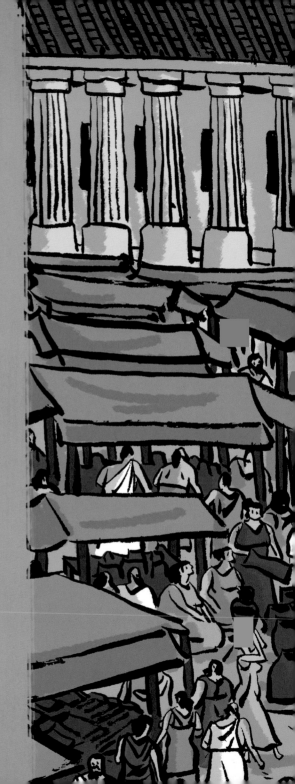

The marketplace and main meeting place in city-states was called the agora. People gathered there to buy and sell goods, attend public meetings, or discuss ideas.

School was part of life for many Greek boys. School started around the age of seven. City-states had different kinds of schools. The city-state of Sparta paid for a military education. It trained boys to become strong and fearless soldiers.

In Athens, families paid to send their sons to school. Students learned to read and write. They memorized famous poems and learned to play an instrument. Schools also taught sports and exercise.

Girls did not usually go to school. Mothers passed their knowledge and skills to their daughters. They learned to cook, weave, and run the house. Some wealthier girls learned to read and write.

Many girls also learned to play musical instruments such as a violin (left) or kithara (right).

Greek children played with rocking horses, spinning tops, rattles, and dolls. They also loved games of running, throwing, and hiding.

15

The Greek people came together for special events. Each year, Athens had two famous drama festivals. The newest plays were performed here. Thousands of people came to see them.

Every four years, Greeks gathered for the Olympic Games. The ancient Olympics were held from around 776 B.C. to A.D. 393. Only men could compete. Women weren't even allowed to watch. The athletes took part in running, wrestling, jumping, and throwing competitions. The winners became heroes in their communities.

Most Olympic athletes wore no clothing.

17

# CHAPTER TWO

# Land of Gods

The Greeks believed in many gods and goddesses. Zeus ruled over all the gods. The eleven other major gods and goddesses were his family. Each one played an important role in life on Earth.

Zeus had two brothers. Poseidon ruled the seas. Hades ruled the world of the dead. Their sister Demeter was the goddess of farming.

Zeus's children also held great powers. Aphrodite was the goddess of love and beauty. Dionysus was the god of wine. Athena was goddess of wisdom and war. Apollo ruled the sun. He was also god of poetry and music.

This statue of Poseidon stands on Kos Island in Greece.

Apollo

Zeus

Poseidon

Dionysus

Athena

Each city-state honored a god or goddess. In return, that god watched over the city. Athens was named after its protector, Athena.

Aphrodite

Demeter

The Greeks built temples to honor their gods. Each temple was for a certain god or goddess. People also honored the gods by sacrificing animals. Most sacrifices took place outdoors on altars. Goats and sheep were the most common sacrifices. Bulls were sacrificed for special events.

Communities celebrated the gods at religious festivals. Often the people walked in a parade. The whole community gathered outside the temple of a god.

Even nonreligious events took place in honor of a god or goddess. The Olympics were held in honor of Zeus. One hundred bulls were sacrificed for him during each Olympics.

There, they offered a sacrifice to the temple's god. The sacrificed animals were then roasted and shared among everyone.

21

# CHAPTER THREE

# City on a Hill

The ancient Greeks invented their own style of architecture, or building design. Greek temples became famous for their design.

Most temples were made from white limestone and marble. The Greeks built temples in the shape of a square or rectangle. Tall columns surrounded the temple's four walls. Each temple had a single room. Inside was a statue of the temple's god or goddess. A city's most important temples stood high on a sacred hill. Most city-states had such a hill. It was called the acropolis, or "high city."

One of the most famous ancient Greek temples is the Parthenon. It has stood on the acropolis at Athens for 2,500 years.

The columns of one temple in Athens were carved into the shape of women. This temple was called the Erechtheum.

The Parthenon took fifteen years to build.

The acropolis in Athens is very famous. It includes several temples in honor of its goddess, Athena. The Parthenon is the largest. Marble for the Parthenon came from 10 miles (16 kilometers) away. Oxen dragged the marble uphill with carts. Workers carved the marble to make thick columns. They cut bricks for the walls. A giant statue of Athena stood inside the temple. The statue's wooden frame was covered with gold and ivory.

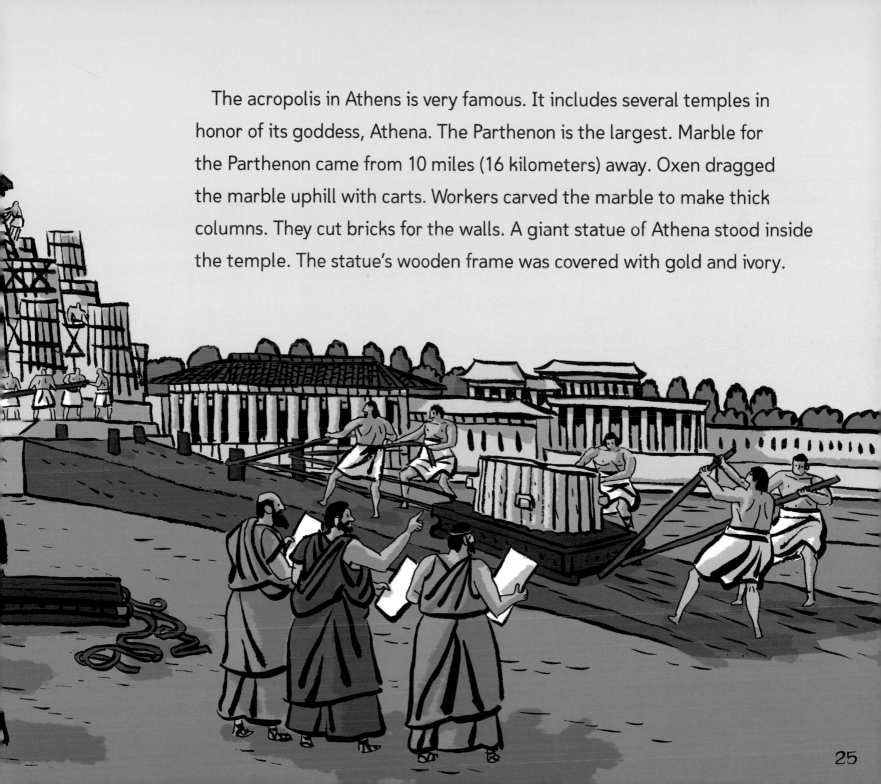

Ancient Greek plays were popular entertainment. They included actors and a chorus. The chorus often sang and danced.

The Odeon of Herodes Atticus is a theater in Athens. It was built into one side of the acropolis. It could seat about five thousand people.

The Greeks also built large outdoor theaters. They dug the theaters out of hillsides. The theaters were shaped like half circles. Rows of stone bleachers surrounded the main stage. These bleachers let people see and hear the play no matter where they sat. Some theaters could seat more than ten thousand people.

# CHAPTER FOUR

# Art, Ideas, and Government

Ancient Greeks loved new ideas. Artists, thinkers, and leaders searched out creative ways to do things.

The Greeks changed the art of sculpture. In the past, sculptures of people had stiff poses and blank faces. Greek artists began to carve statues of people so that they looked real. The sculptures showed the beauty of the human body. The people in the sculptures stood naturally. Their faces showed clear emotion.

*The Discus Thrower is a Roman copy of a Greek sculpture made in about 450 B.C. It shows the movement of an Olympic athlete.*

The Greeks also brought the art of writing to life. Stories were traditionally sung in the form of poems. A poet named Homer is known for two of Greece's first written poems. These famous poems are called *The Iliad* and *The Odyssey*. Some historians believe that Homer was not a real person. They say that a group of poets may have written these poems over time.

Other Greeks were playwrights, or writers of plays. Greek playwrights invented two kinds of plays that are still written today. The playwright Aeschylus wrote the first tragedies. These are serious plays. Aristophanes was a great writer of comedies, or funny plays.

Actors wore masks to perform in plays. The masks projected their voices to the crowd and showed a character's personality.

Some of the world's first philosophers were Greek. Philosophers try to understand the meaning and purpose of life. Greek philosophers used reason, or clear thinking, to understand the world. Three famous Greek thinkers were Socrates, Plato, and Aristotle. Their ideas changed the way people thought.

Aristotle was also one of the first scientists. For example, he studied thousands of animals up close. His work made him the first zoologist, or animal scientist. The ancient Greeks also made important discoveries in mathematics, medicine, and astronomy.

Socrates (*near right*) taught Plato (*far right*) and other men of Athens through speeches and conversations. Plato later wrote down Socrates' ideas in conversations called dialogues.

The Greeks invented the idea of democracy. Democracies let people choose their leaders. Kings and wealthy rulers had controlled Greek communities for hundreds of years. Athens became the world's first democracy about 2,500 years ago.

No one person ran the Athens government. A group of citizens made the city's important decisions. This group was called the Assembly. Any citizen could take part in Assembly meetings. Citizens also voted for their generals. Generals led wars and held much power. But they had to do a good job to be reelected.

This slotted slab was part of a kleroterion. The Assembly used this ancient machine to choose people for public jobs.

Only a small number of Athenians were called citizens. Laborers, slaves, foreigners, and women did not have the right to vote or be part of the Assembly.

# CHAPTER FIVE

# Leading the Way

The greatest leaders of ancient Greece were a lot like our own. They had good ideas. And they knew how to inspire people.

One of Greece's most successful leaders was Pericles. He was a powerful general in Athens from 460 to 429 B.C. Democracy was still new to Athens. Pericles worked hard to encourage this kind of government. His leadership helped make his city-state the most powerful in ancient Greece.

Popular generals like Pericles
were strong speakers.
They had to get the Assembly
to agree to their ideas
and reelect them.

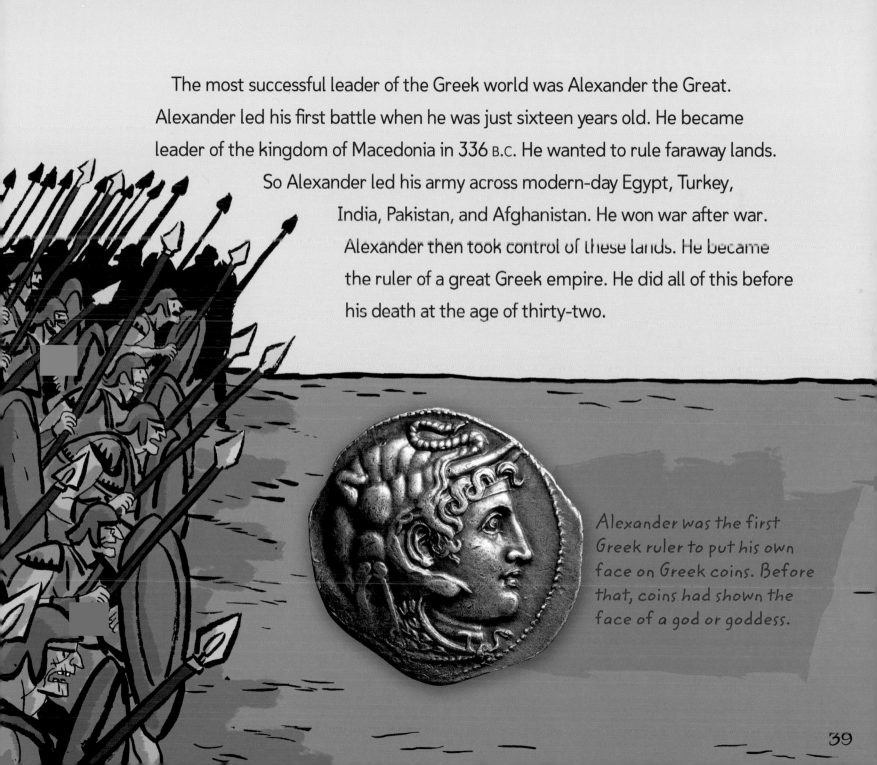

The most successful leader of the Greek world was Alexander the Great. Alexander led his first battle when he was just sixteen years old. He became leader of the kingdom of Macedonia in 336 B.C. He wanted to rule faraway lands. So Alexander led his army across modern-day Egypt, Turkey, India, Pakistan, and Afghanistan. He won war after war. Alexander then took control of these lands. He became the ruler of a great Greek empire. He did all of this before his death at the age of thirty-two.

Alexander was the first Greek ruler to put his own face on Greek coins. Before that, coins had shown the face of a god or goddess.

# CHAPTER SIX

# What They Left Behind

In 30 B.C., the Greek Empire lost power to the Romans. The Romans came from modern-day Italy. The Romans destroyed many Greek buildings, sculptures, and writings. But what survived has inspired people for more than two thousand years.

Modern theater, philosophy, artwork, and architecture are based on examples from ancient Greece. Modern democracies learned from the ideas first formed in Athens. Scientists and mathematicians use Greek discoveries in their work.

The way we write and speak also comes partly from ancient Greece. The Greek alphabet was the first to have symbols for each vowel and consonant sound. Modern alphabets came from this idea.

*Greek soldiers carried round shields in battle and wore armor made of bronze.*

Many ideas from ancient Greece live on today. Yet Greece is a modern country. About 11 million people live there. Its cities are crowded places with tall buildings and busy streets. But reminders of the past are everywhere.

Remains of ancient temples and other buildings can be found across the country. Ancient Greek artwork and writings have survived too. Historians and scientists have studied these pieces of Greece's past. They continue to learn more about the people who lived here so many years ago.

Millions of people visit Greece each year. They come to see the Parthenon, outdoor theaters, sculptures, and other remains from ancient times.

# TIMELINE

**776 B.C.**      The first Olympic Games take place in Olympia around this time.

**700s B.C.**      The Greek alphabet is invented.

     Homer may have written *The Iliad* and *The Odyssey*.

     Greek communities form city-states.

**600 B.C.**      The Greeks begin using coins for buying and selling.

**508 B.C.**      Early democracy begins in Athens.

**497–479 B.C.** Greece fights and wins a major war against a group of people known as the Persians.

**460 B.C.**      Pericles comes to power in Athens.

**432 B.C.**      The building of the Parthenon is completed.

**431 B.C.**      Athens goes to war with Sparta in what becomes known as the Peloponnesian War.

**429 B.C.**      Pericles' rule ends when he dies.

**404 B.C.**      Sparta wins the Peloponnesian War against Athens.

**336 B.C.**      Alexander the Great rises to power and expands the Greek Empire.

**323 B.C.**      Alexander the Great dies.

**146 B.C.**      Greece falls to the Romans.

**30 B.C.**      The Romans take control of the last of Greece's settlements.

**A.D. 393**      The Olympic Games come to an end.

# PRONUNCIATION GUIDE

**acropolis:** uh-CRAH-puh-lihs

**Aeschylus:** EHS-kuh-lihs

**agora:** AG-or-uh

**Aphrodite:** ah-froh-DY-tee

**Aristophanes:** AIR-uh-STAH-fuh-neez

**Aristotle:** AIR-uh-STAH-tuhl

**chiton:** KY-tuhn

**Demeter:** dih-MEE-tur

**Dionysus:** dy-oh-NEE-suhs

**Erechtheum:** ih-REHK-thee-uhm

**Hades:** HAY-deez

*Iliad:* IH-lee-ad

*Odyssey:* AH-dih-see

**Parthenon:** PAHR-thuh-nahn

**Pericles:** PAIR-uh-kleez

**philosophers:** fill-AH-suh-furz

**Poseidon:** poh-SY-duhn

**Socrates:** SAH-kruh-teez

**Zeus:** ZOOS

# GLOSSARY

**acropolis:** "high city" in Greek. This sacred hill was where a city built its most important temples.

**altar:** an outdoor spot where religious sacrifices took place. Many altars were near temples.

**architecture:** the design of a building

**Assembly:** the government organization in Athens that included any citizen who wanted to help make important decisions about the city-state

**chiton:** traditional Greek clothing made from a large piece of cloth pinned together at the shoulders

**city-state:** a community in ancient Greece with its own government and leaders

**class:** a group of people who hold a similar position in a community

**column:** a tall circular support for a building. Columns are usually carved from stone.

**democracy:** a form of government run for and by its people

**drama:** the art of theater and plays

**empire:** a large area ruled by one leader who has total power

**kingdom:** a land ruled by a king

**laborers:** a class of people who did not own land and who worked for pay

**philosopher:** someone who explores the meaning and purpose of life and our place in it

**sacred:** holy or set apart in honor of a god

**sacrifice:** an offering to a god. The Greeks sacrificed animals in return for favors from the gods and protection from harm.

**zoologist:** a scientist who studies animal bodies and habits

# FURTHER READING

Charman, Andrew. *Life and Times in Ancient Greece.* Boston: Kingfisher, 2007. Packed with illustrations and clear text, this book offers helpful information about the history and daily life of ancient Greece.

Donaldson, Madeline. *Greece.* Minneapolis: Lerner Publications Company, 2009. This introduction to the modern country of Greece explores its land, people, and culture through engaging text and photos.

Hart, Avary, and Paul Mantell. *Ancient Greece!: 40 Hands-On Activities to Experience This Wondrous Age.* Charlotte, VT: Williamson Publishing, 1999. The authors offer a fun way to explore the places, people, and historical events of ancient Greece.

Jolley, Dan. *Odysseus: Escaping Poseidon's Curse.* Minneapolis: Graphic Universe, 2008. This graphic novel follows the adventures of Odysseus on his perilous return home after the Trojan War. The story is based on Homer's *The Odyssey.*

Sheldon, Ken, ed. *If I Were a Kid in Ancient Greece.* Peterborough, NH: Cricket Books, 2006. Read this book to find out what it would be like to grow up as a Greek child in ancient times.

Villios, Lynne W. *Cooking the Greek Way.* Minneapolis: Lerner Publications Company, 2002. This book of traditional Greek recipes includes information about cooking during ancient times.

# WEBSITES

Ancient Greece for Kids
http://greece.mrdonn.org
This site is full of information about ancient Greece's history, religion, clothing, people, and more.

Ancient Greece Pictures
http://www.ancient-greece.org/resources/slides.html
This Web page features photographs of Greek buildings, pottery, and sculpture that have survived since ancient times.

The Ancient Olympic Games
http://www.olympic.org/uk/games/ancient/index_uk.asp
This page from the official website of the Olympics features interesting facts about the original games, including a video and a downloadable booklet for students.

Gods and Goddesses of Ancient Greece
http://www.greek-gods.info/greek-gods/
A helpful list of the main Greek gods and goddess includes descriptions and images.

Greece
http://www.timeforkids.com/TFK/specials/goplaces/0,12405,227674,00.html
This colorful, interactive site is full of fun facts about Greece in modern and ancient times.

Odyssey Online: Greece
http://www.carlos.emory.edu/ODYSSEY/GREECE/welcome.html
This fact-filled website includes information about the people, religion, and accomplishments of the ancient Greeks, as well as helpful links.

# INDEX

# PHOTO ACKNOWLEDGMENTS

The images in this book are used with the permission of: © Laura Westlund/Independent Picture Service, p. 4; © The Trustees of The British Museum/Art Resource, NY, p. 10; © Erich Lessing/Art Resource, NY, p. 14; © age fotostock/SuperStock, p. 18; © iStockphoto.com/Gabriela Insuratelu, p. 22; © iStockphoto.com/Bryan Busovicki, p. 26; © Scala/Art Resource, NY, p. 28; © Vanni/Art Resource, NY, p. 30; The Art Archive/Agora Museum Athens/Gianni Dagli Orti, p. 34; The Art Archive, p. 39; © Sean Gallup/Getty Images, p. 42.

## About the Illustrations

Samuel Hiti, who has a background in comic-book art, rendered the illustrations for the Life in Ancient Civilizations series using brush, ink, and computer. Hiti researched each civilization to develop distinct color palettes for these books and create his interpretations of life in these cultures.

Millbrook Press
A division of Lerner Publishing Group, Inc.
241 First Avenue North
Minneapolis, MN 55401 U.S.A.

Website address: www.lernerbooks.com

Library of Congress Cataloging-in-Publication Data

Levine, Michelle.
    The Greeks : life in ancient Greece / by Michelle Levine ; illustrated by Samuel Hiti.
        p.   cm. — (Life in ancient civilizations)
    Includes index.
    ISBN: 978–0–8225–8680–7 (lib. bdg. : alk. paper)
    1. Greece—Civilization—To 146 B.C.—Juvenile literature.  I. Hiti, Samuel.  II. Title.
    DF77.L44  2010
    938—dc22                                                    2008032296

Manufactured in the United States of America
1  2  3  4  5  6  –  DP  –  15  14  13  12  11  10